To

_____

_____

From

_____

_____

For Alicia and Katie,
in memory of Anna Rose,
the sister they never knew, who died at
Great Ormond Street Hospital on
31 December 1997

The Nativity Story

Geraldine McCaughrean

Illustrated by Sophy Williams

LION
CHILDREN'S

Text adapted from *The Jesse Tree* first published by Lion Hudson in 2003.
This text copyright © 2007 Geraldine McCaughrean
Illustrations copyright © 2007 Sophy Williams
This edition copyright © 2007 Lion Hudson

The moral rights of the author and illustrator
have been asserted

A Lion Children's Book
an imprint of
Lion Hudson plc
Wilkinson House, Jordan Hill Road
Oxford OX2 8DR, England
www.lionhudson.com
ISBN 978 0 7459 6092 0

First edition 2007
1 3 5 7 9 10 8 6 4 2 0

A catalogue record for this book is
available from the British Library

Typeset in 18/28 Lapidary 333
Printed and bound in China

Contents

*

Zechariah 6
Luke 1:5-24

Mary   10
Luke 1:26-38

Joseph   13
Matthew 1:18-25

Elizabeth   17
Luke 1:39-44

John   19
Luke 1:57-64

Bethlehem   20
Luke 2:1-7

Shepherds   28
Luke 2:8-15

The Stable   32
Luke 2:16-20

Wise Men   36
Matthew 2:1-8

Three Gifts   41
Matthew 2:9-10

Angels   44
Matthew 2:12-14

Zechariah

*

Zechariah was a man who was happy with his life —
happy with his wife, happy with his work, happy in
his come-day, go-days; happy day and night. There was
just one place, at the heart of him, where he kept a small
dark sadness. Zechariah had no children, and oh, how he
wanted a son!

At the heart of Jerusalem stood a building — vast and
marvellous, ancient and beautiful. Its walls had soaked up
the sunlight of centuries, and inside was a haven of cool
shadow. People came and went all day, meeting friends,
saying prayers, buying offerings, studying the holy
Scriptures. But there was just one place, at the heart of
the Temple, hidden behind a curtain, sunk in a deeper
dark. Only the priests could go there — beyond the curtain
— into the 'Holy of Holies'. Priests like Zechariah.

Zechariah loved the Temple with its soft gloom, its starry candle flames, its heady scent of incense, the quiet babble of voices discussing the Scriptures. Above all, he loved the Holy of Holies. There were memories in there so precious and so ancient that they crammed him topful of wonder and left no room for brooding.

No one but he had any right to be in there. So when Zechariah first saw the figure standing in the shadows, he should have been angry. But he was too startled.

'Greetings, Zechariah,' said the stranger with the candlelit face.

'I don't –'

'Congratulations.'

'For what?'

'You are about to become a father.'

Zechariah almost laughed, almost wept. All his life he and Elizabeth had longed for a child. Now it was far too late. 'Don't make fun of me. I am an old man.'

But the figure, dressed in white and cloaked in sweet-smelling smoke, held up a hand. 'You must call him John. He will herald the coming of the Messiah. He will be a voice shouting for joy in the wilderness!'

At that, Zechariah put a hand to his throat, another to his heart, his aching, thundering heart…

The handful of people praying in the Temple looked up as Zechariah stumbled out from behind the curtain. His eyes were full of candlelight. His hands fluttered like doves. His mouth opening as if to speak… but no words came out. Zechariah had been struck dumb. His fellow priests glanced behind the curtain, to see if some shock, some disaster, some intruder might have caused it, but there was no one, nothing there but a swirl of cloudy incense and candlelight.

Even when Elizabeth, half amazed, half terrified, whispered to her husband that she was expecting a child, Zechariah could only grin like a loon and scratch his joy on a wax tablet using a stylus. His writing looked like angels flying across the white wax.

Mary

✳

Elizabeth had a cousin. Her cousin Mary. Mary was a good girl. Everyone in Nazareth said so when they talked about her – although people probably never talked about her at all. Gossips are only interested in people's faults and mistakes, and Mary did nothing wrong.

She was promised in marriage to the local carpenter, Joseph. The idea pleased her, because it pleased everyone else, and happiness made Mary happy.

It was a warm day, a low sun. The olive trees wore capes of light. The herbs between her fingers gave off a dizzying fragrance. The figure dressed in white, striding along the roadway, reflected the sun so brightly as to dazzle Mary.

'Greetings, Mary,' he said. 'Don't be afraid. God holds you in his mind and in his heart. I have news for you.'

Mary did not jump up or run into the house. She simply greeted the stranger, though she must have been afraid, hearing her name in the mouth of someone she had never seen before.

'The Lord God has chosen you, Mary, to give birth to a son. You must call him Jesus.'

Mary did not faint or laugh, though her face grew paler. 'How can that be? I'm not even married!'

'Mary, you're the most blessed woman alive. God's Spirit will overshadow you. He will entrust you with his own son,' said the angel. 'If you are willing.'

Mary did not protest or cry (though she must have been afraid). She did not speak of the shame her family would feel, the things Joseph would say. She simply lowered her head. 'Let it be as God wishes,' was all she said.

Then the angel was gone, and so was Mary's good name.

Joseph

*

'Expecting a child?' Joseph was appalled. Expecting a child? That spotless, devout, modest young girl everyone spoke so well of? The girl he was supposed to marry? Well, not any more! His chisel dug into the wood as if he were cutting Mary out of his heart. No marriage for him. 'A wife like that you can do without!' said his mother, wagging her head, wagging her hands.

Then Joseph dreamed a dream. It cut into his sleep like the teeth of a saw, it was so real. It burned through his closed eyelids and blinded him, it was so bright.

'Don't be afraid to marry Mary,' said the voice in his dream. *'She has done nothing wrong. The child inside her was placed there by God. He trusts her; so should you. Marry Mary.'*

The dream trickled out of Joseph's head like sawdust from a lathe. But the joy and the fear remained. Joseph lay on his bed staring at the ceiling. He *would* marry Mary: a woman more perfect than even he had realized. But now, of course, she would never be entirely his for, first and foremost, she and the child inside her belonged to God.

And what a responsibility! To raise and clothe and feed and educate the Son of God? A tall order for a simple village carpenter.

Joseph was late opening his workshop that morning.

Elizabeth

✳

Mary went to visit her cousin Elizabeth — the one married to Zechariah, poor man, struck dumb that day at the Temple.

Two women, both expecting babies, both with extraordinary stories to tell. Anyway, pregnant women always have things to talk about: names and worries, clothes and hopes, feeding and fears, sickness, birth and happiness… But even before they met — even as Mary walked up the path to Elizabeth's door — their children were already in touch.

The first Elizabeth knew of her cousin's visit was a riot of joy inside her. Her baby seemed to be leaping and kicking, like a lamb in the spring! Elizabeth hurried outside into the garden, puzzled, but laughing and clutching her sides… And there stood her cousin Mary, smiling.

'He knows! My baby knows! He sensed it!' Elizabeth gasped. 'Mary! Mary! Blessings on you! The blessings of every mother in the world are on you now and on your unborn baby! Feel! Feel! As you came near, the baby inside me sensed it and turned somersaults for pure joy!'

Mary laid her hands on her cousin's stomach. (Her own baby's movements were still too tiny to be felt). It was like a magnet sensing north. It was like a weathercock turning in the wind. It was like the oceans tugged to and fro by the moon. The child in Elizabeth's womb, sensing the closeness of Mary's baby, turned in his watery world and reached out a hand. This other child was calling him to struggle into the light of day. Here was his reason to live.

'Oh Mary!' gasped Elizabeth. 'My baby is jumping for joy!'

John

*

Zechariah's family fretted about him, aging and frail as he was. For nine months now, he had been unable to speak. They just prayed God would spare him long enough to see his son born.

But Zechariah was not sick. He had lost the power of speech, it is true, but not because of any illness. The angel had silenced him — but given him something far more wonderful in return.

One day, his well-meaning neighbours brought him the news — gently, calmly, like a glass of water to a sickbed: 'It's a boy, Zechariah. Your wife has given birth to a son.'

Zechariah wrote wildly on the air.

'Look!' said the neighbours, 'He wants to say something! Fetch the wax tablet and the stylus.'

Then Zechariah wrote: *HIS NAME IS JOHN*.

Like rain falling on a desert, words spilled back into Zechariah's throat. '*His name is John,*' he said, and again and again, '*His name is John. His name is John! His name is John!!*' Then he ran to the window and bellowed it into the street, so that a whole flock of doves flew up from the roof opposite:

'*HIS NAME IS JOHN!*'

Bethlehem

✳

'God will take care of everything,' said Mary, but Joseph was not so sure. The journey could not have come at a worse time. Mary's baby might be born at any time; she ought to be resting at home, not clinging to the lurching back of a donkey mile after tiring mile.

But the Romans (who had recently taken over Israel and started calling it part of the Roman empire) wanted

to count the exact number of people in their newly conquered territory. So they had ordered everyone to travel to their 'place of origin' and register their names. For Joseph and Mary, that meant travelling to Bethlehem, a small town not far from Jerusalem.

The donkey pitched and rolled. As the roofs of Bethlehem came into sight, the unborn baby flexed his muscles. 'It's almost time,' said Mary, biting her lip.

A bed. A bed. Joseph must find somewhere for his wife to rest! But the crowds pushed past like a river breaking round an island. The town was full to bursting! Inside the clattering inn, Joseph had to shout to make himself heard. 'A bed? Do you have a bed for my wife?'

'You are joking, aren't you? Not so much as a shelf! The whole tribe of David is in Bethlehem tonight.'

Joseph's panic rose. If God really was taking care of everything, he did not seem to be making a very good job of it. 'But her child! The baby! It's coming!'

The innkeeper glanced outside at the woman crouched on the ground beside her donkey. 'There's always the stable, I suppose… It's not much, but it's shelter. God be good to you both, my friend. Your baby picked a bad time to be born.'

Across the yard the noise from the inn died down; its lamps went out. The only light in the stable came from a wick floating in a bowl of oil. Its flame danced in the eyes of the animals as they watched Joseph rake together a bed of straw. Their ears tilted; the flies settled on their nostrils, but they went on watching, motionless. For the woman was giving birth, and all animals understand the wonder of that.

There was no snow. Flies yes. Snow no. Flies on the cattle, flies on the donkeys, flies on the dirty straw. All of time was busily fitting itself into a single moment. All of the universe was squeezing itself under a single roof. The maker of the universe was pouring himself into one, tiny, flesh-and-blood human being!

But there were still flies and a smell of dung.

They say the animals spoke on the night Jesus was born. But if they did, they spoke very softly: there was the baby to think of, after all…

Joseph stuffed clean straw into the animals' feed box, and laid the newborn child in that, for a makeshift cradle.

Maybe the stars pulsed overhead, and the planets spun like Catherine wheels, and the moon grinned hugely, and the constellations turned handsprings around the sky.
Or maybe that is how it always feels when a baby is born.

Shepherds

✳

Just up the way – outside town, beyond a fold or two of hills – some shepherds were sitting on a hillside, all huddled up in their cloaks against the midnight cold. They nodded and dozed.

Then all of a sudden, a light fell through the sky: a shooting star – that's what they thought. But the light grew bigger, formed itself into a shape, hurtled down on them, closer and closer. *An eagle after the sheep!* one thought, and fumbled for his slingshot.

Then the light washed over them, and the sheep glowed snowy white in the brightness, and the shepherds folded their arms over their heads and fell on their faces.

'Don't be afraid,' called the figure hanging in mid-air on outstretched wings. 'Wonderful news! Wonderful! The Saviour of the world is born!' The shepherds lifted first one eyelid, then two. The sheep were gazing upwards, too, yellow eyes changed to gold. 'Over there! In Bethlehem! Lying in a cattle manger!' cried the angel. 'Go and see for yourselves!' Within a single beat of his outspread wings, the angel was no longer alone. Others, as numberless as starlings at dusk, were there with him, hovering, silvery and singing, high over the sheepy hill. 'GLORY TO GOD! PEACE TO HIS PEOPLE ON EARTH!' The singing was as loud as cheering, and there was a kind of music, too, as if someone was using the moon for a gong and was jangling all the stars.

Higher and higher the angel flock flew, shrinking to the size and brightness of fireflies. Darkness washed back again over the landscape in a flood. The sheep shuddered.

But the shepherds were already leaping and loping downhill, stumbling into rabbit holes, laughing and shouting out to one another, 'Let's go and see!'

'Yes, yes! Beat you there!'

'Oh no you won't!'

'Wait till I tell the wife!'

'Wait till I tell my children!'

The Stable

✳

Mary was exhausted, but there was not much sleep to be had that night. The baby was no sooner laid in the manger than the shepherds arrived. Sandals slapping in the yard, eyes still full of moonlight, they bundled inside, noisy with excitement – then suddenly clapped their hands over their mouths, dumbstruck.

They hadn't realized it would be like this: a mucky stable, an ordinary family caught in a crisis – people just like them. The baby looked as small and as feeble as any newborn lamb.

And yet for this little chap, that army of angels, those creatures of light, those courtiers from around the throne of God had sung and danced across the sky, dazzling the dark!

Shyly the shepherds explained themselves, twisting their fingers into nervous knots, apologizing. Then they knelt down, before their trembling knees could give way. And their eyes and their minds drank in the wonder of it — that they had been fetched by angels to see this newborn baby king.

Wise Men

*

For as long as people have walked on the earth, they have looked up and seen the stars. The stars were there long before the people. Long, long before: same constellations, same galaxies, same points of light.

But just suppose one night you looked up and saw a *new* star...

And just suppose that brand new star looked back at you – looked you in the eye... and *winked*!

Far away in the East, three astronomers uncricked their necks and stared at one another. 'A new star? What does it mean?' said Casper.

'An omen!' said Melchior, eyes full of starlight.

'Saddle the camels!' said Balthazar. 'We must go and see for ourselves. Someone's been born who's going to change the history of the world!'

The three astronomers took their bearings from the new star and travelled west. Their camels waded through rivers, struggled over dunes, spat at robbers lurking in the dark... During the day, the three sheltered from the sun and from sandstorms, biting mosquitoes, knife-edged winds. But every night they rode on, led by the star, clutching gifts for the newborn king. For surely, someone whose coming warranted a new star in the sky must be an emperor or a king.

Riding into Jerusalem at long last, they made for the palace (of course) and explained their mission to the king who lived there. 'Where is the new king whose birth we have seen written in the stars? We've come a long way to pay our respects to him!'

King Herod only ruled in Israel by permission of the Romans. But he clung on grimly to his crown and his throne and his little bit of power. Now, a pang of anger went through him like an arrow. *New king? New king?*

he thought to himself. '*Surely I am the only king hereabouts!*' But he pinned a smile to his face and said to the three astronomers, 'I'm afraid I know nothing of this star-child. When you find him, *please* come back and tell me, so that I too may… pay my respects.' Under the folds of his robe, his fingers toyed with a dagger in its jewelled sheath. These clever travellers might read miracles in the night sky; but sooner than lose his crown, Herod would gouge out all the stars.

Three Gifts

✳

Finally the star ended its restless journeying – ended it over Bethlehem. The roads were so narrow that the camels had to move in single file. Somewhere a dog barked. Caspar, Melchior and Balthazar wondered if they hadn't made some terrible mistake along the way.

What an exotic sight they must have been for anyone out late that night: three men outlandishly dressed, gabbling in a foreign language and pointing at the stars. What strange noises the innkeeper and his customers must have heard as they turned over in their beds: camels groaning and belching and slumping down onto their knees.

What a strange night for Mary: three dust-stained, wealthy foreigners thrusting gifts at her and her mewing baby. What a strange discovery for the astronomers: two

weary, work-a-day people, a baby in a feedbox, the nervy animals stepping from hoof to hoof. Was it for this that fire had kindled in the distant galaxies, and careered across the measureless canopy of night to announce the birth of a king?

Mary took their presents. A bag of foreign gold. A box of frankincense. (She had smelled that scent before, on the hair and clothes of Cousin Zechariah after a day in God's Temple.) Lastly, the visitors presented a jar of myrrh: a perfume for the dead.

Something for every part of Jesus's life. His birth. His life. His death. From Once-upon-a-time right up to The End.

Angels

✳

Herod waited and waited, digging his dagger into the arm of his throne, ruining the woodwork. What was keeping those three astronomers? As soon as they returned, as soon as he knew where to find that newborn brat… There was one sure way to stop it ever stealing his crown… Tchk, tchk went the dagger's blade into the arm of his chair…

Gathering up their memories, brushing the straw off their robes, Caspar, Melchior and Balthazar camped outside Bethlehem and lay gazing up at the dancing constellations. Happy and weary, they quickly fell asleep.

Suddenly – soft as sheep's wool, white as sheet lightning – an angel came swooping into their dreams.

'Don't go back to Jerusalem! Don't tell King Herod what he wants to know! He would kill the child, not worship at his

cradle. Go home! Go home another way!'

So that's what they did, urging their camels into a gallop, cutting their pack mules loose. Caspar was in such a panic to obey the angel that he never stopped to wonder how he and Melchior and Balthazar had come to dream the selfsame same dream at the selfsame moment. They simply fled, offering up prayers for that helpless little child to the glittering, frosty stars.

The angel in their dreams turned back, meanwhile, flying through the dreams of all Bethlehem that night, until he reached the sleeping Joseph. He had a second message this time for the carpenter from Nazareth.

'Get up, Joseph! You are not safe. King Herod wants the child dead. Make for Egypt, and stay there until the danger is past!'

So that's what Joseph did. The sight did not cause much of a stir: a little family group, with their donkey, crossing an unmarked border into the Egyptian wilderness.

Perhaps they glanced back from time to time, to see if anyone was following, but mostly they looked ahead. Hanging from the saddle's pommel were a pot of gold, a box of incense and a jar of myrrh. Cradled in Mary's arms was the Saviour of the world.

They would be all right, Joseph comforted himself. God would take care of everything… And a good carpenter can pick up work anywhere.

Amazing that he did not notice, following in their wake, all the angels in heaven, numberless as the stars. But then who can tell the size of the angels who watch over us? Are they as huge as condors, the size of larks or small as the grains of dust kicked up by a donkey's hooves?